Copyright @ 2019 by Debbie J Hefke
Published by Debbie J Hefke Copyright @ 2019

All rights reserved. No part of this publication may be reproduced, distributed, or transmitted in any form or by any means, including photocopying, recording, or other electronic or mechanical methods, without the prior written permission of the publisher, except in the case of brief quotations embodied in critical reviews and certain other noncommercial uses permitted by copyright law.

Printed in the United States

Acknowledgements

To Tom Hayes for helping me create this book and working on the writing of these Pete story's.

Special thanks to Lizzete Duvenage Super artist.

By Debbie Hefke

"Bye, Mom," said Pete the Polar Bear. "Bye, Ms. Bear." Said his best friend, Sally. Pete and Sally watched Ms Bear jump on an ice patch and paddle away. Today was the first day of fishing. She promised to bring home dinner.

Before Ms. Bear was out of sight, Sally and Pete entered Pete's den. Sally reached in her backpack and pulled out two pieces of her favorite bubble gum. Sweet and Sour Sardine. "Have some BUBBLE GUM, Pete" said Sally. Pete looked puzzled.

"Gee, Sally. I think Mom said bears shouldn't chew gum, especially, BUBBLE GUM."

"Don't worry, Pete. BUBBLE GUM never hurt anyone."

Pete and Sally each put the gum in their mouths. Pete struggled. The gum moved side to side, up and down, and back and forth. The sweet and sour taste filled his mouth with saliva.

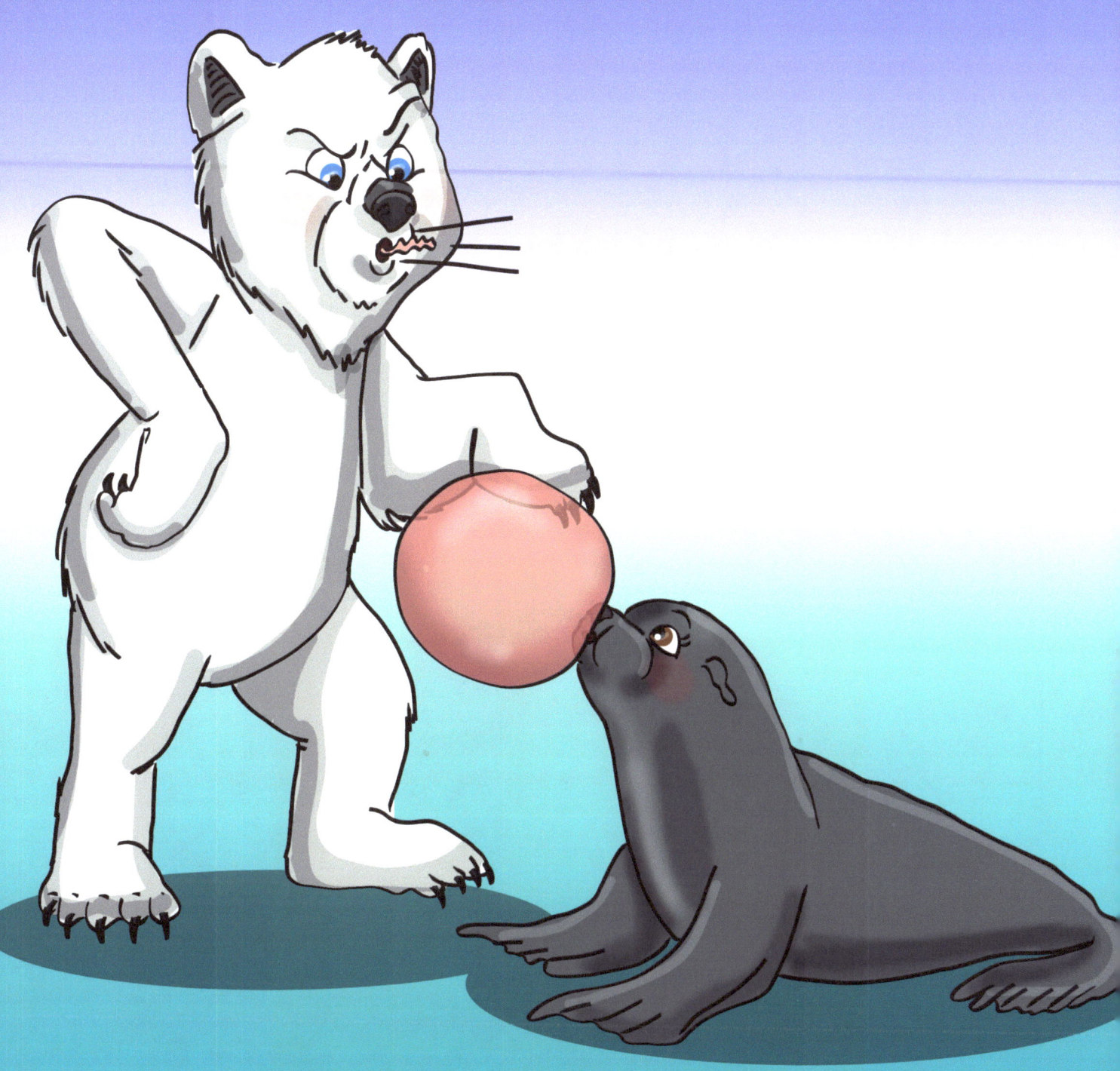

As the bubble grew, Sally clapped and barked. "Wow, Pete, that's terrific!"

The bubble grew and grew. Sally was no longer able to see Pete.

"This won't end well, I should duck for cover."

She looked for cover. As soon as she hid beneath the area rug, the bubble burst.

Sally heard a. . .

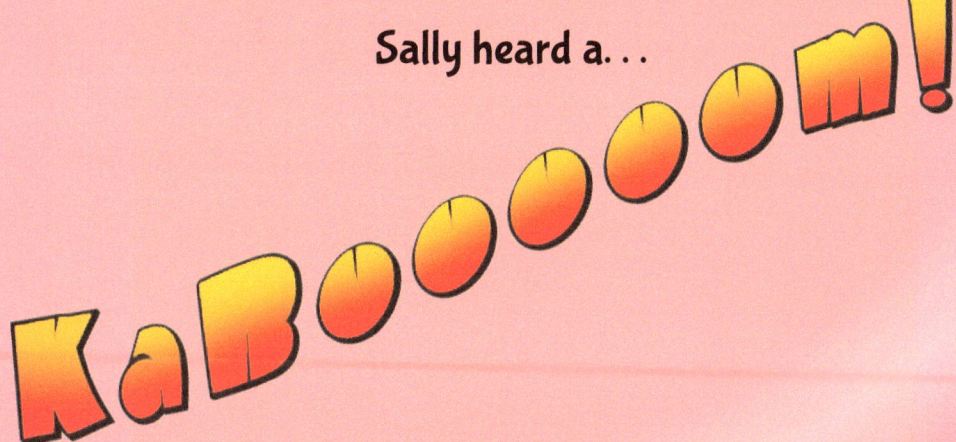

Then a loud, liquid, smacking sound hit things all around her.

Pete roared in terror!

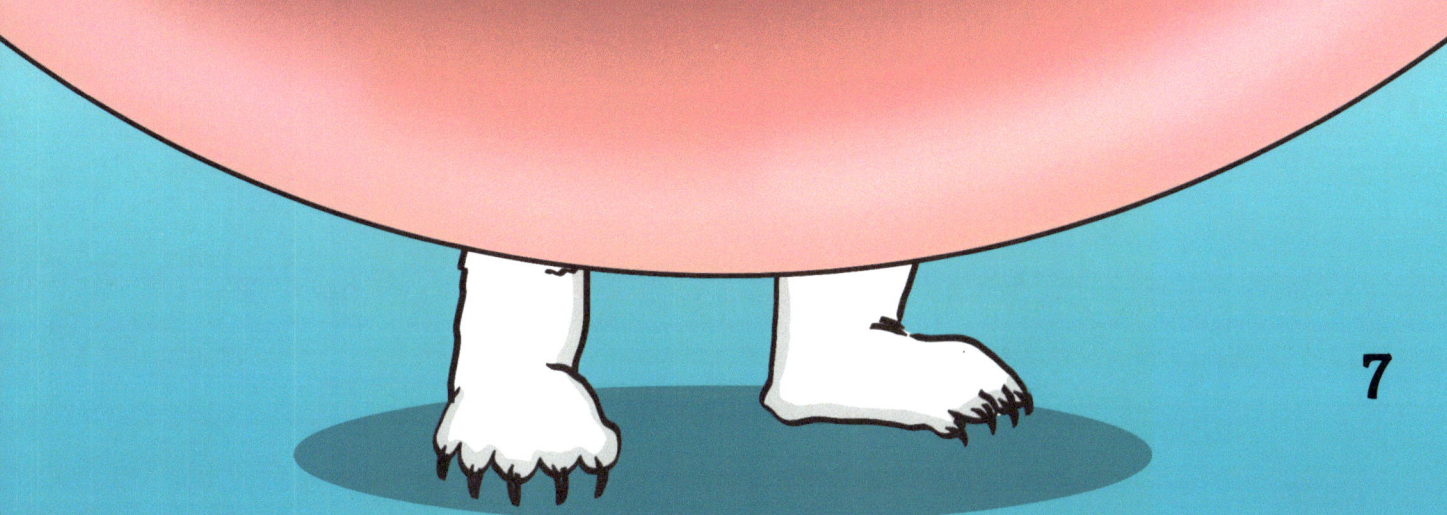

The walls and the ceiling of the den were now dripping with gum. Pete was covered in BUBBLE GUM. Laying on the floor blinking, not sure what just happened Pete **struggled** to sit up. Sally under a rug and safe. She started to laugh.

"Oh no Pete, your mom is going to be mad."

Pete was a mess. "Gee, Pete, you know, maybe, bears shouldn't chew BUBBLE GUM," said Sally. Pete was too **sticky** to speak.

"What's my mom going to say?" Asked Pete.

Sally slapped her head and thought.
"Boy, Pete, you're in trouble."

Sally snickered as Pete swung his BUBBLE GUM covered paws around.

Pete roared, "Sally, do something!"

Sally scrambled for anything to solve Pete's problem. **Searching** the house for items. Sally balancing tomatoes on her nose, when she came back in the room ready for BUBBLE GUM removal.

Sally grabbed Ms. Bears **fur dryer**, plugged it in, and fired it at Pete. The gum got hot, stickier and began to melt even more over Pete's body.

Next, she placed tomatoes and cucumber slices on the sticky spots.

"Sally, I feel like **pizza**," said Pete.

"Sally, this isn't working," roared Pete. "That's why I'm using **ice cubes**, Pete. I want to freeze the gum, then we can peel it off."

"But Sally I hate the cold".

When the ice cubes melted and the gum remained, Sally dug a hole and stuck Pete inside. "**Just roll**, Pete. The **dirt** should work."

When the dirt didn't work. Sally tried Ms. Bear's **tweezers**.

Pete grunted, "Sally this hurts worse."

When the tweezers fizzled, Sally turned to **scissors.**
"Now Pete hold still, this won't hurt a bit." Sally smiled. Pete clenched his teeth holding very still, wondering if this will ruin picture day next week.

Pete and Sally never heard Ms. Bear enter the den. Sally looked at Pete's startled mom and said, "Gee, Ms. Bear, how was the **fishing?**"

Ms. Bear wasted no time. She grabbed a **Jar of peanut butter** and slathered Pete head to toes. Sally grinned, "boy Pete you look delicious all we need now are some crackers".

When the tomatoes, cucumbers, peanut butter, and gum were gone, Pete and Sally learned a valuable lesson. If a bear is going to chew **BUBBLE GUM** he needs to wear a raincoat and hat.

It was a bright and beautiful sunny day and Pete and Sally decided to try chewing BUBBLE GUM again. Sally smiled as she blew a bubble. Pete was just about to start blowing his bubble When!

Find out what happens to Pete in the next book.
Pete's Chilly Experience

The End

Wooden Leg Productions
Coming soon

Pete's Chilly Experience

Pete's Water Test

Pete's Visit at Grandpaws

Pete's First Fishing Class

Pete's Hairy Cuts

www.ingramcontent.com/pod-product-compliance
Lightning Source LLC
Chambersburg PA
CBHW042019090426
42811CB00015B/1689